BREAKOUT BIOGRAPHIES

SIMONE BILES

Greatest
Gymnast of
All Time

Caitie McAneney

New York

Published in 2018 by The Rosen Publishing Group, Inc.
29 East 21st Street, New York, NY 10010

First Edition

Editor: Elizabeth Krajnik
Book Design: Tanya Dellaccio

Photo Credits: Cover Alex Livesey/Getty Images Sport/Getty Images; cover, back cover, pp. 1, 3, 4, 6, 8, 10, 12, 14, 16, 18, 20, 22, 24, 26, 28–32 ninanaina/Shutterstock.com; p. 5 Robert Beck/ Sports Illustrated/Getty Images; p. 7 (top) A. RICARDO/Shutterstock.com; pp. 7 (bottom), 11 (both), 21 (top), 23 (top) Leonard Zhukovsky/Shutterstock.com p. 9 Joe Scarnici/Getty Images Sport/Getty Images; p. 13 (top) TOSHIFUMI KITAMURA/AFP/Getty Images; p. 13 (bottom) Lintao Zhang/ Getty Images Sport/Getty Images; p. 15 Dean Mouhtaropoulos/Getty Images Sport/Getty Images; p. 17 (top) Laurence Griffiths/Getty Images Sport/Getty Images; p. 17 (bottom) Clive Brunskill/ Getty Images Sport/Getty Images; p. 19 (top) Tim Clayton - Corbis/Corbis Sport/Getty Images; p. 19 (bottom) David Ramos/Getty Images Sport/Getty Images; p. 21 (bottom) BEN STANSALL/AFP/ Getty Images; p. 23 (bottom) Jean Catuffe/Getty Images Sport/Getty Images; p. 25 (top) Maddie Meyer/ Getty Images Sport/Getty Images; p. 25 (bottom) LEON NEAL/AFP/Getty Images; p. 27 (top) EMMANUEL DUNAND/AFP/Getty Images; p. 27 (bottom) Kevin Mazur/WireImage/ Getty Images; p. 29 Michael Loccisano/Getty Images Entertainment/Getty Images.

Cataloging-in-Publication Data

Names: McAneney, Caitie.
Title: Simone Biles / Caitie McAneney.
Description: New York : PowerKids Press, 2018. | Series: Breakout biographies | Includes index.
Identifiers: ISBN 9781508160700 (pbk.) | ISBN 9781508160724 (library bound) | ISBN 9781508160717 (6 pack)
Subjects: LCSH: Biles, Simone, 1997–Juvenile literature. | Gymnasts–United States–Biography–Juvenile literature. | Women gymnasts–United States–Biography–Juvenile literature.
Classification: LCC GV460.2.B55 M367 2017 | DDC 796.44092–dc23

Manufactured in China

CPSIA Compliance Information: Batch Batch #BS17PK: For Further Information contact Rosen Publishing, New York, New York at 1-800-237-9932

CONTENTS

A TRUE CHAMPION

Simone Biles is one of the greatest athletes in the history of gymnastics. Her strength and **showmanship** have caught the attention of people around the world. She was one of the most talked-about athletes to compete in the 2016 Summer Olympics in Rio de Janeiro, Brazil. At only 19 years old, she took home five Olympic medals.

Perhaps one of Biles's most notable features is her height. At only 4 feet and 9 inches (1.4 m) tall, she was the shortest gymnast on Team USA. However, Biles makes her small body work in her favor. Using great strength, she pushes through **complex** gymnastics **routines**. Biles has shown the world that it's not the size of the athlete that matters, but the amount of **determination** and skill they bring to their sport.

Simone Biles completes difficult gymnastics routines in a way that seems effortless.

BORN TO BE A GYMNAST

Simone Biles was born in Columbus, Ohio, on March 14, 1997. When she was three years old, Biles went to live with her grandparents in Spring, Texas. Her sister, Adria, went to live in Texas, too. Ronald and Nellie Biles adopted the girls and became their parents. They made a huge difference in the girls' lives.

Biles showed gymnastics talent from a very young age. She would do backflips and other gymnastics moves at home. When she was only six years old, she went on a field trip to a gym called Bannon's Gymnastix. Young Biles watched as gymnasts worked out and practiced their routines. She tried to do those moves herself. Biles was soon hooked on gymnastics.

Biles started training to be a gymnast soon after her field trip to Bannon's Gymnastix.

FINDING A COACH

Simone Biles's gymnastics skills grew quickly. Soon, a coach named Aimee Boorman noticed Biles's skills. The two started working together when Biles was around seven years old. Since Boorman had never coached an **elite** athlete before, Biles and Boorman learned about the world of elite gymnastics together.

In 2014, Ronald and Nellie opened the World Champions Centre in Spring, Texas. This huge gym is where Biles trained with Boorman until the 2016 Summer Olympics.

Just weeks after the 2016 Olympics ended, Boorman announced that she was leaving the World Champions Centre to become director of women's gymnastics and elite coordinator at EVO Athletics in Sarasota, Florida. She promised to be there for Biles whenever Biles needs her.

Biles said that Boorman has been like a "second mom" to her.

GYMNASTICS EVENTS

Gymnastics competitions consist of four different events. Like all gymnasts, Biles had to learn how to compete in each event. One event is the vault. Gymnasts run at full speed towards a **springboard**. They spring off the board with their hands and flip and turn over the vault **apparatus** in order to land on the other side. One goal is to "stick the landing," or land with both feet on the ground.

Another event is the balance beam. Gymnasts turn, jump, flip, and perform **handsprings** on the balance beam. The goal is to perform without falling off or wobbling on the beam.

Gymnasts also perform on uneven bars. This event includes two raised bars several feet from one another. One is higher than the other. Gymnasts swing, flip, and

Each gymnast is different and may do well in one or more events. Biles's greatest challenge may be the uneven bars. However, she is a master of the floor exercise.

FLOOR EXERCISE

The floor exercise is one of Biles's best events. This event allows gymnasts to show their personalities through music and dance. The gymnast performs handsprings, twists, and **saltos** with grace. She has to run to gain **momentum** for flips and handsprings. Biles has amazing leg strength. She uses her momentum to perform many gymnastics moves.

FAIL OR FIGHT

Biles began to compete in national competitions in 2010. At the Women's Junior Olympic National Championships that year, she won gold in the floor exercise event. In 2011, Biles started to compete at the elite level.

In 2013, Biles performed at a competition called the U.S. Classic. She made so many mistakes that she started to doubt herself. She didn't even finish all of her events. She said, "I just thought it was the end of the world."

Biles decided to see a sports **psychologist**. She was a master of the physical part of competing, but she had to work on the mental part. One thing was for sure—Biles was not ready to give up on her career.

The year 2013 was a year of growth for Simone Biles. It wasn't always easy, but she never gave up.

GOING GOLD

Simone Biles worked to show the world that she was ready to compete seriously when she performed at the P&G Gymnastics Championships in 2013. The P&G Championships are the national gymnastics championships for the United States. In gymnastics, the all-around winner has the highest combined score from all of their events. This winner is considered the best gymnast in the country. In 2013, Biles won that all-around gold medal.

At the 2013 World Championships, Biles won the all-around gold. She was the first African American woman to do so. The national and world events that year gave Biles the confidence she needed to succeed. Her win at the 2013 World Championships was a breakout moment for Simone Biles.

Simone Biles stands with her gold medal at the 2013 World Championships.

RISING
TO FAME

Biles put all of her energy into every competition she entered. A string of victories followed. Soon, she began to rise to even more fame in the gymnastics world.

In 2014, the Women's Sports Foundation named Biles Sportswoman of the Year. She also won all-around gold at the World Championships for the second year in a row. She won four gold medals, as well as a silver medal for vault.

Biles continued her success in 2015. She won U.S. all-around gold, as well as all-around gold at the 2015 World Championships. Biles even beat Gabby Douglas, the winner of the all-around gold medal at the 2012 Summer Olympics, at the World Championships. At this point, Biles had earned more world championship medals than any other U.S. female gymnast in history.

Between 2013 and 2016, Biles won all-around gold in every competition she competed in.

"THE FLYING SQUIRREL"

Gabby Douglas rose to world fame at the 2012 Summer Olympics in London. She was the first African American to win the all-around individual title in the Olympics. She was also the first American to win a gold medal in both the individual all-around event and the team all-around event. Douglas's best event is the uneven bars. In fact, she was nicknamed the "Flying Squirrel" because of her ability to fly from bar to bar.

Rio2016

"THE BILES"

   Not many gymnasts have a gymnastics move named after them. However, when Simone Biles completed a very difficult move in 2013, people took notice. The move became known as "The Biles," as she was the first person to complete it in a world competition. The International Federation of Gymnastics added "The Biles" to its Code of Points. The Code of Points is a rulebook for gymnastics that defines how each level of the sport is scored.

   "The Biles" involves a double layout, or two backward flips in the air. It also involves a half twist out, which is a twist in the air. In addition to these moves, "The Biles" also involves a blind landing, or a landing where the gymnast can't see the ground as she approaches it. How does Biles pull off this move? She has to run very quickly to gain momentum. Then she pushes off with her feet and gets enough height to complete the double layout and the half

Some people think Biles's move goes against the laws of **physics**. Her height and her very strong leg muscles work together to make this move possible.

19

TEAM USA

Simone Biles was too young to compete in the 2012 Olympics. That meant her Olympic **debut** would have to take place in 2016. As the top all-around gold medalist for the United States and the whole world, Biles was likely to make the U.S. women's gymnastics team. She was on her way to the Olympic Trials.

The Olympic Trials for U.S. women's gymnastics were held in San Jose, California, in July 2016. Biles competed against 13 other female gymnasts. Only five women could be part of the U.S. Olympic team.

Biles won first place in individual all-around, vault, and floor exercise for both nights of the competition and was named to the U.S. women's gymnastics team. Her teammates included Gabby Douglas, Aly Raisman, Laurie Hernandez, and Madison Kocian.

ALY RAISMAN

Aly Raisman began gymnastics when she was two years old. She was not new to the Olympics when she joined the women's gymnastics team in 2016. Raisman also competed in the 2012 Summer Olympics in London. She took home three medals, more than any other American gymnast in that Olympics. After the 2012 Olympics, Raisman took a year off from training. She returned to the 2016 Olympics, where she won one gold medal and two silver medals.

Simone Biles stands with the other members of the 2016 U.S. women's gymnastics Olympic team.

SUCCESS
IN RIO

Even before Biles went to Rio, people in the gymnastics community were looking forward to her Olympic debut. Soon people outside of the gymnastics community would also know who Simone Biles was. It wasn't long into the Olympics before she became a household name.

In team all-around competitions, the coach decides which team member is the strongest gymnast for each event. Biles competed in all events—vault, uneven bars, balance beam, and floor exercise—for the team all-around finals. She led the U.S women's gymnastics team to victory.

Biles also shone in her individual events. She won the gold medal for individual all-around. That means she earned the highest combined score for all the events in the women's individual all-around event at the Olympics.

Aliya Mustafina from Russia (left) and Simone Biles (center) and Aly Raisman (right) from Team USA accept their medals for the women's artistic gymnastics individual all-around event at the 2016 Summer Olympics in Rio de Janeiro.

THE FINAL FIVE

At the 2012 London Olympics, the U.S. women's team called themselves the "Fierce Five." For the 2016 Rio Olympics, the U.S. women's gymnastics team chose the name "Final Five." The nickname honored U.S. women's gymnastics team coach Martha Karolyi, who retired later that year. They were the final five gymnasts she would coach at the Olympics.

SHATTERING

RECORDS

Simone Biles gave it her all in each of the events she competed in at the Olympics. In fact, the only event in which she did not win a medal was the uneven bars. She went on to win a gold medal for vault and a bronze medal for the balance beam. It came as no surprise that Biles also won first place in her best event—the floor exercise.

By the time the 2016 Olympics ended, Biles had won five medals, and four of those were gold. She is one of only five female gymnasts in the world who have won four gold medals at a single Olympics. Biles left Rio de Janeiro as one of the most decorated athletes. She became a worldwide celebrity over the course of two weeks.

Simone Biles holds the American flag at the closing ceremonies of the 2016 Summer Olympics in Rio de Janiero, Brazil.

USA FOR THE WIN!

The 2016 Olympics were a great victory for the United States. Individual athletes and teams won 46 gold medals, 37 silver medals, and 38 bronze medals. The United States won 121 medals in all. That was 51 more medals than China, which took home the second-highest number of medals. The United States's top medal winners included Biles, swimmers Katie Ledecky and Michael Phelps, and sprinter Allyson Felix.

WHAT'S NEXT?

Simone Biles left the 2016 Olympics with more than gold medals. She left with the attention of the whole world. People wanted to know, "What will Biles do next?" She had to decide whether to retire or to continue training before the next Summer Olympics.

After the Olympics, Biles and her coach, Aimee Boorman, parted ways. Biles decided to take a break from training for a while, and she said she wasn't sure what her next step would be. She said that she was looking forward to being a normal teenager and doing things such as eating pizza, watching Netflix, and spending time at the pool. After years of competing and training for the Olympics, Biles was ready for a quieter life.

After the Olympics, Biles went on tour with her team. She gave many interviews. The "Final Five", with the exception of Gabby Douglas, presented Beyoncé with the award for best female video for her song "Hold Up" at the 2016 MTV Video Music Awards.

GETTING TO KNOW SIMONE

What is Simone Biles really like? In many ways, she's just like any other young person in America. She says her favorite kind of food is Italian food. Her favorite books are the *Hunger Games* books and her favorite music is whatever's popular on the radio. She enjoys hanging out with her friends and going shopping. Her patriotic glitter eyeliner from the Olympics showed the world that she is a big fan of sparkles.

Biles may enjoy ordinary things, but she is an extraordinary athlete. She showed the world her talent again and again at worldwide championships and became one of the brightest stars at the 2016 Olympics. Whether or not she continues to compete, Biles has left her mark on the gymnastics world forever.

Simone Biles will go down in history for her amazing gymnastics skills.

TIMELINE

March 14, 1997 — Simone Biles is born in Columbus, Ohio.

2010 — Biles wins gold for her floor exercise routine at the Women's Junior Olympic National Championships.

July 2011 — Biles places first on balance beam and vault and third all-around at the U.S. Classic.

2012 — Biles switches to homeschooling so she can train more.

July 2013 — Biles has a rocky performance at the U.S. Classic.

October 2013 — Biles wins all-around gold and other medals at the World Championships in Antwerp, Belgium.

October 2014 — Biles wins all-around gold and other medals at the World Championships in Nanning, China.

July 2015 — Biles wins all-around gold and other medals at the U.S. Classic.

October 2015 — Biles wins all-around gold at the World Championships. She becomes the first woman to win three consecutive world gymnastics titles.

October 2015 — Biles joins Team USA for the 2016 Summer Olympics in Rio de Janiero, Brazil.

August 2016 — Biles wins four gold medals at the 2016 Summer Olympics in Rio de Janeiro, Brazil.

GLOSSARY

apparatus: The equipment gymnasts use to compete.

complex: Having many parts.

debut: A first public appearance.

determination: A quality that makes you continue to do something that is difficult.

elite: Being part of the highest level.

handspring: A movement in which you jump backward or forward, land on your hands, swing your legs up and over, and land on your feet.

momentum: The force that something has when it is moving.

physics: The branch of science that deals with matter, energy, force, motion, and the relationship among them.

psychologist: Someone who studies and practices the science of the mind and behavior.

routine: Movements that are repeated as part of a performance.

salto: A flip or roll, usually in the air.

showmanship: The ability to perform in an entertaining way.

springboard: A strong, flexible board that is used to help athletes

INDEX

WEBSITES

Due to the changing nature of Internet links, PowerKids Press has developed an online list of websites related to the subject of this book. This site is updated regularly. Please use this link to access the list:
www.powerkidslinks.com/bbios/biles